Endorsements for the Church Questions Series

"Christians are pressed by very real questions. How does Scripture structure a church, order worship, organize ministry, and define biblical leadership? Those are just examples of the questions that are answered clearly, carefully, and winsomely in this new series from 9Marks. I am so thankful for this ministry and for its incredibly healthy and hopeful influence in so many faithful churches. I eagerly commend this series."

R. Albert Mohler Jr., President, The Southern Baptist Theological Seminary

"Sincere questions deserve thoughtful answers. If you're not sure where to start in answering these questions, let this series serve as a diving board into the pool. These mini-books are winsomely to-the-point and great to read together with one friend or one hundred friends."

Gloria Furman, author, *Missional Motherhood* and *The Pastor's Wife*

"As a pastor, I get asked lots of questions. I'm approached by unbelievers seeking to understand the gospel, new believers unsure about next steps, and maturing believers wanting help answering questions from their Christian family, friends, neighbors, or coworkers. It's in these moments that I wish I had a book to give them that was brief, answered their questions, and pointed them in the right direction for further study. Church Questions is a series that provides just that. Each booklet tackles one question in a biblical, brief, and practical manner. The series may be called Church Questions, but it could be called 'Church Answers.' I intend to pick these up by the dozens and give them away regularly. You should too."

Juan R. Sanchez, Senior Pastor, High Pointe Baptist Church, Austin, Texas

How Can I Love
Church Members
with Different
Politics?

Church Questions

How Can I Love Church Members with Different Politics?, Jonathan Leeman and Andy Naselli

What If I Don't Desire to Pray?, John Onwuchekwa

What If I'm Discouraged in My Evangelism?, Isaac Adams

What Should I Do Now That I'm a Christian?, Sam Emadi

Why Should I Join a Church?, Mark Dever

How Can I Love Church Members with Different Politics?

Jonathan Leeman and
Andy Naselli

WHEATON, ILLINOIS

"What do you think, Simon? From whom do kings of the earth take toll or tax? From their sons or from others?" And when he said, "From others," Jesus said to him, "Then the sons are free."

Matthew 17:25–26

May the God of endurance and encouragement grant you to live in such harmony with one another, in accord with Christ Jesus, that together you may with one voice glorify the God and Father of our Lord Jesus Christ. Therefore welcome one another as Christ has welcomed you, for the glory of God.

Romans 15:5–6

It was the Sunday after a presidential election. I (Jonathan) had been teaching an adult Sunday school class on Christians and government that fall. The church, like most of the nation, was still absorbing the result of the election's unexpected outcome. And feelings that morning were raw.

I began the class by talking about sympathy. I wanted to encourage members whose candidate had won on Tuesday to sympathize with members whose candidate had lost. Christian maturity, I observed to the class, knows how to both disagree with someone and yet still show compassion. An older minority woman whose candidate had lost raised her hand and said that she had not felt any sympathy from the church and that she was scared. Minutes later, a middle-aged white woman raised her hand and said she was astonished at my call for sympathy because the losing side was "evil."

At that moment—you can be sure—I second-guessed my decision to teach that class that morning.

Yet those two women offer us something very honest: a picture of how challenging it can be to love people with different political opinions, even when they are members of the same church.

This question is what we want to address in this book: *How can we love fellow church members when we disagree on political matters?*

Make no mistake: Andy and I are writing this booklet because we need it too. We can both think of moments that highlight our own challenges to love when political topics arise. Moments like:

- Avoiding that guy who always wants to talk about his political hobbyhorse.

- Regarding that woman condescendingly because she just feels too far right or too far left.
- Feeling like that fellow member is the enemy, maybe not even a real Christian, because he voted for the other side.

Such feelings can arise whether viewing people to our right or to our left on the political spectrum.

Why We Feel Skeptical or Angry toward Fellow Members amid Political Differences

Our concern here is not with the mild disagreements, ones that don't affect the heart's posture toward someone else. Rather, we're interested in the disagreements that affect your heart's posture or that hinder fellowship with another person in your church. Maybe you feel scorn. Maybe you are angry that they support a cause that you are convinced is unjust. You might even find yourself questioning their profession of faith: "How can they be Christians and support *that*?!"

We can think of at least three reasons such skepticism arises in our hearts amid such disagreements.

Reason 1: Justified People Care about Justice

The work of government is fundamentally con-
cerned with matters of justice, and people who
have been justified by Christ—Christians—care
about justice. They care about *righteous judgments*, which is one way to define justice from
the Bible. It makes sense, therefore, that you
would ask questions, even become skeptical,
when Christians choose what appears to be a
path of injustice. They appear to be making unrighteous judgments.

Let's unpack all of this. God instituted gov-
ernments to establish a basic platform of justice
for everyone created in his image (Gen. 9:5–6;
2 Sam. 8:15; 1 Kings 10:9; Prov. 29:4; Rom.
13:1–7). That means all those conversations
you have with friends and colleagues about
the election, abortion, immigration, poverty,
same-sex marriage, criminal-justice reform,
America's trade policy with China, or party
membership are conversations fundamentally
about justice.

Furthermore, anger is the God-given emo-
tion for responding to injustice. If you hear of a

child being abused, you should be angry. Anger's purpose, after all, is to oppose. We Christians should all oppose injustice. So think again of your conversation with fellow church members over the election or immigration or welfare policy. When they disagree with you, your instincts tell you they are choosing injustice. They are recommending unrighteous judgments, and that can make you angry.

If it's a particularly significant issue, it can even tempt you to question their standing in the faith. Why? Think about it like this. James tells us that true faith creates good deeds and that good deeds demonstrate our faith. Our good works prove that our faith is genuine: "I will show you my faith by my works," he says in James 2:18 (see the diagram below).

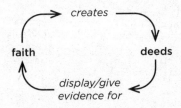

Which means, when deeds are absent, we lack evidence for faith. James even questions the faith of someone who demonstrates no deeds: "You believe that God is one; you do well. Even the demons believe—and shudder!" (James 2:19). Like Jesus said, "You will recognize them by their fruits" (Matt. 7:16, 20). Are you with us so far?

Now, instead of saying *faith* and *deeds*, let's substitute *justification* and *justice*, which offer another way of getting at the same ideas. In the same way that faith creates deeds, so God's work of justifying a person by grace through faith creates a concern about justice. And in the same way that deeds display and give evidence of faith, so our concern for justice demonstrates and gives evidence for our justification (see the diagram below 2).

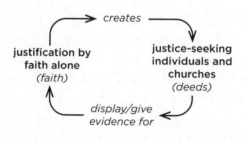

It's a virtuous cycle, if there ever was one.

Now let's pull everything together. Politics involves questions of justice. When fellow Christians disagree with you on significant political matters, you question their commitment to justice, which in turn can sometimes tempt you to question their justification. We're not saying you're always *right* to do so. We're merely saying it *makes sense* that this happens. There are theologically correct instincts at play. Plus, every once in a while, such questioning *is* right.

For now, let's consider the next reason we may feel skeptical.

Reason 2: Self-Justifying People Are Certain Their Convictions Are Just

We are tempted to scorn and second-guess our fellow church members whose politics disagree with ours because every one of us is naturally self-righteous and self-justifying, and fallen politics is fueled by such self-righteousness and self-justification.

Part of Adam and Eve's decision to disobey God and eat the forbidden fruit was convincing themselves that eating the fruit was a just act. Ever since, we have been self-justifying creatures. Adam's bite of the fruit and Pharaoh's spilling of blood are the same thing: self-justified acts of self-rule.

Now, people may often be right in their opinions and in their politics, but that's not what we're talking about here. We're talking about the basic posture of the fallen heart to always think that it's right—to always think its cause is just. Even as children, we would get into fights with our siblings over dolls and trucks because we were convinced our causes were just. *But Mom, he hit me first!* When we were born again, wonderfully, we lost the need to justify ourselves before God through our personal and political pursuits. Christ became our justification. Whenever we walk in the Spirit, then, we become able to seek out the plank in our own eye, not just the speck in our neighbor's eye, and to fight for what's right, not to justify ourselves but for the sake of love. Born-again politics is a different kind of politics.

The challenge is that we are presently located at a moment in the Bible's storyline of redemption where we find ourselves simultaneously justified and sinful. We are capable of walking by the flesh and the Spirit both. As authors, therefore, our goal is to help you be a little more theologically self-aware. Are you convinced about your own political opinions? If so, maybe that's because you are walking in the Spirit, you love your neighbor as yourself, and you have rightly formed judgments about the issues of the day. Then again, it also might be because you are following the self-justifying script of every other political party, of every other tribe and nation, throughout the history of the world.

All this means that the anger you feel when people disagree with you politically might be the right response to injustice. But remember God's word: we must be "slow to become angry, because human anger does not produce the righteousness that God desires" (James 1:19–20, NIV). Too often we use our anger as a weapon to destroy anything that opposes our personalized version of a just universe. We're self-serving with our anger.

To summarize reasons 1 and 2, our anger and skepticism toward fellow church members with different politics makes sense, but it may not be as righteous as we think it is. We give with one hand what we take away with the other.

Still, all of that is pretty theological. It's this next reason that forces us to start getting into the practical weeds.

Reason 3: Political Judgments Require Wisdom

Most political judgments we make depend on wisdom not on directly applying explicit biblical principles. To put this another way, there is some space between our biblical and theological principles and our specific political judgments. Two Christians might agree on a biblical or theological principle but disagree on which policies, methods, tactics, or timing best uphold that principle. Why, then, are political disagreements so difficult? Because we lack wisdom!

What is wisdom? It's a capacity of mind that combines the fear of the Lord with the skill of living in God's created but fallen world in a way that yields justice, peace, and flourishing. It looks to God's word, yes, but it also takes stock of circumstances, people, and all the knowledge

available to all people through common grace.
Wisdom recognizes that there's a time to build
and a time to tear down, and it's always asking,
"What time is it now?"

Think of King Solomon when the two
prostitutes each claimed that a baby was hers.
There was no biblically scripted solution to his
dilemma. He had to think about it. If he had
asked his counselors, they would have advised
different solutions. Yet Solomon knew what to
do: offer to divide the baby in half with a sword,
which in turn exposed the real mother and the
imposter. Solomon's solution, the narrator con-
cludes, was wise: "And all Israel heard of the
judgment that the king had rendered, and they
stood in awe of the king, because they perceived
that the wisdom of God was in him to do justice"
(1 Kings 3:28). The goal was justice; the means
was wisdom.

Now pick any contested political issue of our
own day, such as the controversy surrounding
Central and South American asylum seekers and
other migrants crossing the southern United
States border. One group of Christians believes
the present laws are just fine. If anything, they

believe we need to tighten the restrictions in order to protect our nation and our children. Another group of Christians argues that humanitarian considerations mean allowing as many migrants in as the present law allows or even changing the laws to accommodate more. And let's agree that "protecting our children" and "showing compassion to asylum seekers" are both biblical impulses. Still, there's a long way to travel between affirming those two biblical principles and determining how to balance them in public policy. How many migrants should a nation permit a year? How many asylum seekers? How will that affect the economy and people's livelihoods? What is the best way to prevent and combat drug and human trafficking? Is a nation obligated to undertake all the costs of processing the hundreds of thousands of migrants who might show up at the borders? What kinds of housing conditions should refugees have at the border? What about child-parent separation? What unintended consequences might follow this decision or that decision?

You might know your personal answers to those questions. But can we admit these are tough questions whose answers rely on wisdom-based political judgments, not explicit biblical principles? As we said a moment ago, there is some space between those political judgments and our biblical and theological principles. Political judgments depend on figuring out how to apply our biblical and ethical principles to the vast and complex set of circumstances that surround every political decision. They account for social dynamics, legal precedents, political feasibility, historical factors, economic projections, ethnic tensions, criminal-justice considerations, and so much more.

People today often treat their votes as personal expressions of who they are. Yet we would encourage you to view votes less as matters of self-expression or tribal identification and more as strategic calculations concerning these kinds of non-biblical matters. Then recognize that different Christians will make different wisdom-based calculations.

Here's another example. We hope you agree with us that abortion is murder, which Scripture forbids. Our shared opposition to abortion is grounded in the wisdom of God. But that's different than agreeing on political tactics for overcoming abortion. Some Christians take an incrementalist strategy. They advocate for policies that prohibit abortion with the exceptions of rape and incest because they think such policies stand a better chance of passing. Others think an incrementalist strategy like this is compromising, and they adopt an all-or-nothing approach. Still others insist on adding "whole life" considerations to our opposition to abortion. Who is right strategically? It's hard to be certain, of course, because here we're relying on our own wisdom. The Bible has principles to bring to bear, but it doesn't speak directly to political tactics like that.

Beyond all of this, if you want to get things done in a democratic system, you have to make alliances with people with whom you don't agree on everything. That's why political parties exist. There are just not enough people who think exactly alike on every issue. Therefore, we have to join together with people who agree with us on a significant clump of issues in order to get anything done.

The trouble is, this process of alliance building or party formation brings moral considerations into play. Are we morally culpable for
any evil legislation the other members of our
political party manage to push into law? What
if the other party does even more evil? Is our
only choice then disenfranchisement? Does it
make a difference if the evil we're talking about
is a "small evil" versus a "big evil"—and how big
is "big"? This much is certain: we need wisdom!

Notice also how quickly the ground shifts be-
neath our feet. Suppose you lived in Germany in
the early 1920s, and a Christian friend told you
he joined the National Socialist German Workers
Party—the Nazis. You would have misgivings,
but you probably wouldn't feel certain enough to
excommunicate or ban him from your church. By
the early 1930s, however, those misgivings would
have grown considerably, and you would want
to discuss the topic of excommunication, as evi-
denced by the 1934 Barmen Declaration in which
the Confessing Church publicly denounced all
Nazism. And then, how much more certain
would you be by the 1940s? The point is, life and
politics are not static, and with every passing day

we need a fresh dose of wisdom because the political landscape keeps changing. Christians will have different opinions all along the way.

Looking at the landscape in the United States today, some Christians seem untroubled by their choice of party. Others don't feel fully aligned with either party and say they hold their noses and pick "the lesser of two evils." Still others wonder if one or both of the major parties have become off-limits for Christians, as was the situation with the Nazi Party. Personally, we would be shocked if any political party ever felt like a perfect fit for a Christian, as that just might suggest one's Christianity has been subverted by party thinking. Nor do we believe in moral equivalency—some parties are better than others, and some injustices are worse than others.

Yet our goal throughout this booklet is not to offer you our assessments of the political landscape or to tell you which political judgments to make on any given political matter. Rather, it's first to encourage you to ask God for wisdom, and second, to remind you that neither you nor your fellow church members are Solomon, much less Jesus, who alone is perfectly wise. Remem-

bering this should create *some* room for charity
and forbearance.

How Can We Love Church Members with Different Politics?

Put these three reasons together, and what do
you get? Frustration. On the one hand, we know
we should be united in the gospel and our views
about justice. We serve the same King! On the
other hand, we have different ideas about how to
serve our King. Jesus has not returned, perfected
us, and given us complete wisdom. So for one
reason or another, our judgments diverge. Theo-
logians might call this an "already/not yet" pickle.
We've *already* been saved, but we've *not yet* been
perfected. We don't want to bicker, but we do.

With all that in mind, how can we love
church members with different politics? Here
are six recommendations.

Recommendation 1: Adjust Your Expectations

Let's start with this last point—the fact that we
live in an "already/not yet" moment of redemp-
tive history. If you find a church in which the

members think exactly like one another politically, you might rightly wonder how that happened, especially if the church is economically, generationally, ethnically, or nationally diverse.

The gospel does not automatically resolve all our wisdom-based political judgments in the here and now. It helps us love and forbear with one another amid those different wisdom-based judgments. It creates unity amid diversity, not uniformity.

If you look around and notice that your church is politically uniform, you might ask, Where did it come from? Are there non-biblical pressures to conform to certain class, generational, ethnic, or political-party standards? Is something (besides the gospel) creating that uniformity? If so, might those cultural standards be wrongly binding consciences about what Christians must believe?

Here, then, is a big irony: even if your church is healthy, your members will likely not be entirely uniform in their politics. Your members might even feel some measure of political tension. What unites them is Jesus, not partisan politics.

Unity amid diversity, furthermore, can be a strength of a church's witness to outsiders. You want outsiders to see your church and think, *Wow, you guys love one another across political divides! I've never seen anything like that!* Sadly, we're more likely to be known for our strident tone.

Picture Jesus walking around with his disciples. In the group were both Matthew the tax collector and Simon the Zealot. Talk about different politics! Furthermore, there's no reason to think both Matthew and Simon abandoned their political opinions of Rome entirely. Even if following Jesus softened their opinions, one might have remained more bothered about Roman occupation while the other remained less bothered.

Recommendation 2: Recognize What a Church Is

Building on the last point, recognize what a church in the Bible is. Jesus did not design our churches to be a national or ethnic or class gathering or the gathering of a political party. Rather, he designed them to be gatherings of his followers from every tribe and tongue and nation.

Your church and ours are communities of former enemies learning to love one another. They are communities of political rivals working together.

We are natural-born enemies. Each of us wants to rule. The "dividing wall of hostility" separating Jew and Gentile separates all of us (Eph. 2:14). Yet, just as God made Jew and Gentile "one new man" through his work on the cross (Eph. 2:15), so he makes us all one (Eph. 4:4–6). Members of every other nation, race, and tribe learn to live as fellow citizens of Christ's kingdom —a new nation and new race (1 Pet. 2:9).

There's been nothing like the church in the history of the world. Every other nation has been united either by powerful men with swords or by family relations, including ancient Israel. Yet now a new nation exists, held together by neither sword nor family but only by Word and Spirit. Indeed, it's a nation that doesn't presently possess a land. It's like God wanted the world to see what he alone could do. So he took a bunch of natural enemies, saved them by his Son's blood and his Spirit's power, and created a united and peace-sharing people.

The local church is where enemy tribes start

beating swords into plowshares and spears into pruning hooks. It's where black and white, rich and poor, young and old, educated and uneducated, American and Chinese, sanitation worker and senator, unite.

What does all of this mean practically for you? It means you show up at the church's gathering on Sunday knowing your job is to beat those swords into plowshares. You expect to encounter that guy who rattles on and on about his political hobbyhorse, or that couple who aligns themselves differently than you, and you recognize that these encounters are good and God-intended. We're not saying you necessarily abandon your own perspectives, but that you listen and you love. You have an opportunity to lower your sword and show the world another kingdom created by supernatural power.

Recommendation 3: Recognize What Unites a Church and What Belongs to the Domain of Christian Freedom

If Jesus did not design our churches to be gatherings of citizens or political parties but of

Christians, an obvious question follows: What exactly does unite a church? The answer to that will help us know what to do with our political disagreements and how seriously to take them. Can people who disagree on tax rates be united in a church? What about disagreements over abortion?

Remember what we said earlier about space existing between our theological principles and our political judgments. Another way of getting at the same idea is to recognize the line between what we will call *whole-church issues* and *Christian-freedom issues*. This is crucial, so it's worth taking more time to explain.

Whole-church issues are those issues that unite a church and make a church a church—issues such as the gospel, our entire statement of faith, an affirmation of repentance, and participation in the ordinances. Whole-church issues are the things that we as a church agree a Christian must believe or practice—as in, "Christians must believe the gospel; Christians must repent of sin; Christians must be baptized," and so forth.

Meanwhile, Christian-freedom issues are those issues that may be important and morally significant, even tremendously so, but that we're not quite ready to say "Christians must" with them. By no means is this the realm of moral relativity. Still, we won't treat these things as conditions for church membership (or salvation) because we want to leave space for Christians to disagree inside of our church.

Christians will disagree about which issues fall on which side of the line. Some say a particular view on baptism is a whole-church issue; others don't. Some say a certain stance on the millennium (premil? amil? postmil?) is a whole-church issue; others don't. Fine. Our point here is that a line does exist. To borrow language from Jesus, some things a church will bind, while other things it will loose (Matt. 16:19; 18:18). The church will decide that "belief *x*" or "practice *y*" is necessary for being a Christian and church membership, or that it is not.

Furthermore, we hope we can all agree that everything on the whole-church side of the line should be explicitly biblical or clear "by good and necessary consequence" (to use a phrase from the *Westminster Confession*). Churches should not bind the consciences of members on an issue as a condition for membership unless the Bible teaches it. The Pharisees were known for binding consciences where Scripture didn't, and so are cults. We don't want to repeat the errors of either. Therefore, before we impose our convictions on others, we always want to use two criteria: "Is this something I'm convinced Bible preachers should preach as Bible, and is it so clear in Scripture that we should treat it as a criterion for church membership?"

For instance, we both personally believe the divinity and humanity of Christ are whole-church issues, while the nature of the millennium is not. We believe calling people to repent of sexual immorality is a whole-church issue, while encouraging people to homeschool their children is not. Some issues on the Christian-freedom side of the line might be really close to the line. Other issues are farther away. You know you've crossed the line into the whole-church domain when the belief or practice becomes possible grounds for removing someone from membership in the church as an act of discipline (or excommunication). For example, our churches would excommunicate a member for denying the divinity of Christ or for unrepentant sexual immorality.

None of this is to say that people won't have biblical convictions on the Christian-freedom side of the line. You might be convinced from the Bible that an amillennial view of the end times is accurate. But you might simultaneously decide that this is not worth placing in a church's statement of faith because it's not something for Christians to divide over. You can happily come to the Lord's Table with somebody who shares a premillennial view. I (Jonathan) even remember once sharing my understanding of the millennium in a Sunday school class that I was teaching. I also told the class that my perspective was not in the church's statement of faith and that people could disagree with my understanding of Scripture on this topic and still be happy members of our church. Except for the most diehard advocates of one perspective or another, this concession lowered the emotional temperature around the topic of the millennium considerably. While our consciences must always be bound by Scripture, I wanted the class to know that our church had never decided to put its weight behind a certain view of the millennium like it had put its weight behind a first-tier issue like Christ's divinity or even a second-tier issue like baptism. Our church would bind consciences on first- and second-tier issues. It would not bind consciences on a third-tier issue like the millennium.

That was a lot of explanation. Now let's return to politics. How does recognizing this distinction between whole-church issues and Christian-freedom issues help us to love church members with different politics?

The short answer is, we are saying you must keep this distinction between whole-church issues and Christian-freedom issues super clear in your mind when it comes to discussing politics. When Christians lose track of the distinction, they risk tearing apart a friendship, a small group, even a church. A whole-church issue, after all, can legitimately warrant excommunication. You don't want to unthinkingly treat Christian-freedom issues as if they are whole-church issues that warrant excommunication. When we do that, we begin to divide ourselves from our brothers and sisters with the quiet thought inside our head, *How can they be Chris-*

tians and think that?! or *They must be immature or thoughtless Christians!*

When you are tempted to think that way about, say, political topic x, pause. Collect yourself. Now think carefully: Is political topic x a whole-church issue? Do you really think the preacher should preach your perspective on topic x as *the* Christian position? Do you expect him to open up his Bible and preach on topic x as a conscience-binding application of Scripture for every Christian? Also, do you believe that your church should excommunicate anyone who believes the opposite of you on topic x? Or should your church screen people with a question about topic x when they try to join your church, just like you might ask people to explain the gospel?

It's not always obvious whether an issue falls on the whole-church or Christian-freedom side of the line. Really complicated issues might break down into parts that fall onto both sides of the line. Still, the line exists, and the vast majority of political issues, tactics, and strategies are Christian-freedom issues. With Christian-freedom issues, you are free to discuss them with fellow members. You are free to work at persuading friends. You can even, in a very light-handed way, treat such issues as a discipleship matter, particularly if the issues are complicated but morally significant. But if you do, you must do it with tremendous sensitivity and care. One way or another, you must communicate with your words, your tone, even your body language, that "You can disagree with me, and our fellowship and friendship will in no way be jeopardized. We are brothers and sisters in Christ." This is what I (Jonathan) did when I told the Sunday school class that my view of the millennium was not in the church's statement of faith. Both Andy and I are extraordinarily careful to do this whenever discussing politics.

In fact, by acknowledging that an issue is a Christian-freedom issue, you should be able to say to yourself, "I don't *need* to discuss this, and my Christian fellowship with this person who disagrees with me will remain as strong as ever." You should be able, as it were, to change the subject.

Yes, this can be really, really hard. After all, a political conversation is a conversation about what is just. This is not simply Wheaties versus Cheerios. These are morally significant conversations. But still, if you are able to admit to yourself that people in your church should not be removed from membership for disagreeing with you, then you must practice love and forbearance. You might be right, and they might be wrong, but you must practice love and forbearance. Your political judgment does not reach either a sufficient level of biblical clarity or a level of moral significance to make it a whole-church issue. So loosen your grip and lower the emotional temperature. Being able to do this, when the occasion calls for it, is a sign of Christian maturity.

Perhaps it would be helpful to illustrate topics on both sides of the line. Suppose it's the late 1950s, and a lawyer in your church is working to uphold some vestige of the Jim Crow laws, which segregated black people from whites. With the benefit of hindsight, we today believe that such laws were evil. Meaning, we wish more preachers would have preached against them and that churches would have disciplined from membership people like this lawyer. Churches should have treated it as a whole-church issue. Sadly, many churches failed to recognize this at the time. After all, churches should unite around repentance from discrimination and bigotry. (Let's pray that God would give us such moral clarity about the issues facing us today.)

But now consider something like tax policy. Suppose two members of your church get into an argument over whether or not it's fair to impose steep taxes on the wealthy. One member says, "I think the rich should pay their fair share."

The second member replies, "Fair by what standard? Fair by the standard of your coveting what the wealthy have?"

The first rejoins, "Hey, I'm just trying to side with Jesus, who said, 'Everyone to whom much was given, of him much will be required'" (Luke 12:48).

The second reacts, "Do you intentionally manipulate the Bible to justify your opinions, or are you just ignorant?" As you can probably guess, this conversation will not turn out well.

Aside from the immaturity and rudeness

on display here, we would want both parties to recognize that the tax-rate questions at play here belong on the Christian-freedom side of the line not the whole-church side. Yes, imposing a steeper tax on the wealthy is a morally significant matter, one that we cannot brush off as unimportant. Yet we propose that it's difficult to open our Bibles and address it with as much clarity and certainty as we can address the principles in our churches' statements of faith. We would not encourage preachers to exhort members to adopt one position or another or to discipline any members who disagree.

Instead, these two church members need to stop and consider the source of their unity: the gospel and their commitment to the Bible broadly. They need to recognize that this is not a whole-church issue and that, at the end of the day, they can agree to disagree on this topic. They also need to find better ways of discussing their differences.

When are the biblical principles at stake clear enough to call something a whole-church issue? That brings us to the next recommendation.

*Recommendation 4: Determine Whether
an Issue Requires a Straight-Line or
a Jagged-Line Judgment*

How can we know when a political issue belongs on the whole-church or Christian-freedom side of the line?

There is no simple "always this" or "always that" answer to that question. Again, Christians will disagree. Perhaps it will help to dig a little deeper into the kind of judgment we're making with a whole-church issue versus the kind of judgment we're making with a Christian-freedom issue.

In short, a whole-church issue depends on straight-line judgments, while a Christian-freedom issue depends on jagged line-judgments.

By saying whole-church matters depend on straight-line judgments, we mean that there is a simple straight line between a theological or ethical principle found in the Bible and a political conviction (see the diagram opposite). Think back to the abortion illustration. The Bible says, "You shall not murder." It also says that God knew us in our mother's womb. We believe mov-

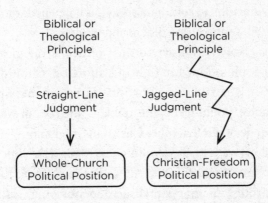

ing from these two biblical texts to the political issue of abortion involves a straight line. If murder is wrong and if an unborn baby is alive inside the mother, then abortion is wrong. Preachers and churches, therefore, should take a stand on abortion, both in their preaching and in their membership decisions. Churches should excommunicate anyone who unrepentantly promotes abortion, whether personally by encouraging women to seek them or politically by advocating for the cause. Though we do not affirm the gospel faithfulness of Roman Catholic churches, we do appreciate the occasional news report of a Roman Catholic bishop denying some politician admission to communion, as has happened with Ted Kennedy, Joe Biden, and others.

Now let's move to the political strategies people adopt for fighting abortion. Should Christians picket abortion clinics? Jonathan and I would feel comfortable doing so, but we understand that other Christians might not. We don't want to make willingness to picket a clinic a test of faithfulness. After all, the decision to protest an abortion clinic depends on a host of judgments that are *not* necessarily a straight line from Scripture: Is such a protest arguably more effective than other forms of opposition? Do protests risk hardening the hearts of abortion advocates? Does faithfulness require such protest no matter how people respond? On and on the questions could go.

Here's another example of a jagged-line judgment. Suppose a Christian wants to argue for universal health care as a human right. He might start with an ethical claim about human rights as a biblical idea, but from there the argument has to move back and forth down a jagged path, satisfactorily answering multiple questions on which Christians might reasonably disagree.

What services would be covered? At what cost to the taxpayers? What would the economic trade-offs be, and are those just? What if standards of care dramatically drop, such that more people cannot receive life-saving treatment? With questions like these and so many others, it would be harder to assert that universal health care is *the* Christian position and that church membership decisions should be made accordingly. Rather, the topic belongs in the domain of Christian freedom and belongs to the individual Christian conscience. Christians can have strong convictions for or against universal health care. But they must not make those convictions a standard of Christian faithfulness and treat anyone who disagrees with them as sub-Christian or as a less mature Christian.

I (Jonathan) remember once asking an acquaintance if he thought Jesus agreed with his positions on health care and tax policy. This person confidently replied that Jesus did. He believed he held *the* Christian position or *the* biblical position on health care and tax policy.

Let's stop and think about what it means when we talk as this man did. We are saying this is what the Bible teaches and that all Christians must adopt our position in order to obey Scripture. We are saying we can be as confident in that political position as we are in the claim that God gave the Ten Commandments to Moses or that Jesus walked on water.

Too often we fail to realize how our political conversations as Christians should be different than the political conversations of non-Christians. Non-Christians can tell you exactly *what they think*. Christians can too, but the crucial difference is that Christians can also tell you—on some political topics—*what God thinks*. We have his Book. He has revealed himself. That's amazing, isn't it? Yet a huge danger looms. We get into a political argument in which we're telling someone *what we think*. But we also have a Bible in our hands, and so we begin to blur the lines between *what we think* and *what God thinks*.

You know how it works. You feel strongly about something. You can quickly find a Bible passage or two to back you up, and you begin to talk as if God agrees with you (see Matt. 15:9).

You might think you're exempt from this danger. But we dare to say that we've all done this at one time or another. In fact, we can point to two thousand years of Christians misusing the Bible to justify their preferred political outcomes, and we humbly suggest that we're not any smarter or wiser than all of them.

To avoid confusing our thoughts with God's thoughts, therefore, we must treat God's Book with holy reverence and fear. We must take great care to distinguish its authoritative and inerrant wisdom from our own. To help with that, Jesus established local churches. The very existence of a local church, whose job is to mark who the Christians are on Planet Earth, requires us to have one set of criteria for whole-church issues and another set for everything else. It requires us to distinguish between straight-line and jagged-line judgments.

Recommendation 5: Respect Your Brothers and Sisters Who Have a Differently Calibrated Conscience on Jagged-Line Judgments

But, what happens when you think a political matter involves a jagged-line judgment and a fellow church member thinks it depends on a straight-line, whole-church judgment? This recently happened in my (Andy's) church when a godly church member requested that the elders preach on climate change. He argued that humans are causing global warming, that global warming is bad, and that this issue is categorically on par with the sanctity of life. Here's how I attempted to gently respond to that brother:

> On the one hand, we must be responsible stewards of God's creation. Recklessly damaging God's creation is sinful. On the other hand, there are certain issues on which Christians must be able to disagree. What are the best strategies for addressing care for God's creation in our American context? Some people are convinced that humans are causing global warming and demand that we significantly rethink how we live in order to be faithful stewards. Others—some for a complex variety of good reasons—are not convinced that humans are causing global warming or that global warming is neccessarily bad and are cautious to insist on specific applica-

tions (e.g., install solar panels on the roofs of your buildings and don't drive SUVs). How exactly we should steward creation is a complex issue because it depends not only on how we interpret specific Bible passages but on how we interpret data outside of Scripture. And individual Christians interpret the data outside of Scripture differently.

Our jagged-line judgments yield what Paul calls "disputable matters" or "matters of conscience." We just distinguished between whole-church matters and Christian-freedom matters of conscience. Let's further unpack what a matter of conscience is.

Your conscience is your consciousness of what you believe is right and wrong. That implies that your conscience is not necessarily correct on every issue. What *you* believe is right and wrong is not necessarily the same as what *God* believes is right and wrong. You might believe with deep conviction in your conscience that a five-year-old boy has the right to choose to become a biological female. If so, we would argue that your conscience is not functioning correctly for that issue because it is based on immoral standards according to Scripture. We would argue that you should calibrate your conscience.

The idea of *calibrating* your conscience suggests that your conscience is an instrument. Instruments can be incorrect: your bathroom scale may say you weigh 187 lbs. when you actually weigh 182 lbs.; your car odometer may indicate that your speed is 62 mph when it's actually 58 mph; your watch may say the time is 8:52 p.m. when it's actually 8:54 p.m. When an instrument is incorrect, it'd be nice if someone calibrated it. To calibrate an instrument is to align it with a reliable standard to ensure that it's functioning accurately.

The standard for what's right and wrong is God, who has revealed himself to us particularly through the Bible. So when your conscience is not functioning accurately, you should endeavor to align it with God's words. The classic example of this in the Bible is the apostle Peter. He was convinced in his conscience that it was sinful to eat certain foods—like bacon. God told Peter *three times* to "kill and eat" animals that Peter considered to be unclean. Peter had the gall to reply to God, "By no means, Lord; for I have never eaten anything that is common or unclean." But because *the Lord* was commanding Peter to eat those foods, Peter had to recalibrate his conscience so that he would have the confidence to accept food and people that he previously could not accept (Acts 10:9–16).

So how should you calibrate your conscience? In three basic ways:

1. *Calibrate by educating it with truth.* Truth refers primarily to the truth God reveals in the Bible, but it also includes truth outside the Bible. For example, the decisive information that may lead a Christian couple to use or not use a particular form of contraception may be truth outside the Bible—that is, scientific information that explains in detail how a form of contraception works.

2. *Calibrate in the context of your church.* Godly church leaders and fellow members are one of God's gifts to you to help you calibrate your conscience. You don't have to do it alone.

3. *Calibrate with due process.* Some issues may take you years to work through. That's okay.

It's better not to rush the calibration than to prematurely change and go against your conscience.

How does all this relate to jagged-line judgments? It's critical that Christians distinguish between straight-line, whole-church issues and jagged-line, Christian-freedom issues because the consciences of Christians should function differently with them. For straight-line, whole-church issues, pastors should preach, "This is what God says." It's right to try to persuade people to be conscience-bound on whole-church issues.

Jagged-line, Christian-freedom issues are matters of conscience on which fellow church members should be able to agree to disagree. Romans 14:1 calls these issues "opinions" (ESV) or "disputable matters" (NIV). Disputable matters include issues such as how you interpret who "the sons of God" are in Genesis 6 or how Christians should view the Sabbath. It also includes the vast majority of political judgments. For example, is the American government presently enforcing the death penalty in a just way? If not, what are the next steps the government should take to solve that problem?

Keep in mind that jagged-line judgments easily become deeply ingrained in your conscience, and that sets the scene for conflict because we inevitably *dispute* disputable matters. No two sinful humans agree on absolutely everything—not even a godly husband and godly wife. We have different perspectives, backgrounds, personalities, preferences, thought processes, and levels of understanding of truth about God, his word, and his world. So it's not surprising when fellow church members disagree about jagged-line judgments. We should expect that and learn to live with those differences. We don't always need to eliminate such differences, but we must seek to glorify God by loving each other in our differences. That is Paul's main concern in Romans 14.

We'll highlight just two of Paul's principles from Romans 14:

1. *Welcome those who disagree with you as Christ has welcomed you* (Rom. 14:1–2; 15:7). When you encounter those who have a weak conscience on a theologically incorrect but not heretical issue, your main priority should not be for them to change their view. After all, the

issue is not "of first importance" (1 Cor. 15:3). Your main priority is to "welcome one another as Christ has welcomed you, for the glory of God" (Rom. 15:7).

2. *Don't look down on those who are stricter than you on a particular issue, and don't be judgmental toward those who have more freedom on a particular issue* (Rom. 14:3–4). Love those who differ with you by respecting them, not disdaining them. Don't assume that anyone who is stricter than you is legalistic or that anyone who is freer than you is licentious. When you are convinced that a certain political strategy is just, you may be tempted to treat it as a matter of first importance, but that would be a grave mistake because it would imply that those who disagree with you on that issue cannot be Christians.

So is it okay to talk about jagged-line issues with fellow Christians? Yes, but only if you do it with the right spirit and the right proportion. Be strict with yourself and generous with others. Don't become so preoccupied with jagged-line issues that you are divisive about them. Jagged-line issues should not be so important to you that they're all you want to talk about.

Recommendation 6: Remember What's Most Important

Working for justice is important. It's one part of Christian discipleship. Christ's justified people care about justice. Yet it's worth noticing what the New Testament emphasizes as the best means for pursuing a just world. It emphasizes making disciples.

Just think about the epistles. They are not primarily tracts on how to do justice outside of the church. They are primarily tracts on living justly and righteously inside the church. Our political engagement outside should flow out of our justice- and righteousness-seeking lives inside. Jesus, Paul, and the rest of the apostles could have spent a lot of time talking about Caesar and the political world of that day. They did say a few things but not much.

So it's not that Christians shouldn't care about justice. It's that we know any good "the upcoming election" will do, at best, will be temporary and full of holes, and we desire a perfect justice that will last. Which is precisely why Christians join together as churches. The straight-line judgments and whole-church matters that unite us point to the perfect justice that will last. All the jagged-line, Christian-freedom issues we spend so much time debating will not last, at least not as clearly and crucially.

It's not surprising that non-Christians view the next election as THE MOST IMPORTANT THING IN THE WORLD!!! They work themselves into a feverish pitch, as if heaven and earth hang in the balance. It becomes a form of worship. Christians should know better. We are not utopians. Ancient Rome came and went. The Holy Roman Empire came and went. The Soviet Union came and went. Even your nation will come and go, no matter which nation you name as your own. As has been said, sometimes the best way to critique the present system and to resist the false worship that so much of politics demands is simply to talk about something else.

Jesus will win. His kingdom does not hang in the balance. Christians who possess this happy confidence can engage with one another amid these secondary political matters while simultaneously enjoying unity and fellowship and hope as they together anticipate the coming of Christ's perfect reign.

Working for Justice, Loving the Justified

More and more, the two of us find ourselves in conversations with brothers and sisters in Christ who feel stuck. They "cannot possibly imagine" voting for *this* party or *that* party or *either* party.

Our goal throughout this booklet has not been to resolve those tensions or to render those judgments for you but to clarify what's at stake in our fellowship together. In fact, the more a nation denies God, we predict, the less savory all our options might be. Like our brothers and sisters in Communist China or Muslim Iran, Christians in the democratic West might increasingly discover what disenfranchisement feels like. It's not just in the public square that Christians feel challenged with ethical dilemmas; it is in the schools and the workplaces too: "Can we send our child to this public school?" "Do I attend the mandatory office engagement party for the same-sex couple?" "Do I include my preferred gender pronouns in my email signature line when my department chairman insists I must?"

As the culture presses hard against the church, unfaithful compromise will always be one threat. Yet Mark Dever has observed that there is another threat that conservative Christians should watch out for: *balkanization*, or dividing into a hundred pieces. One Christian says we "must" this; another that we "must" that; a third calling down curses on both houses, along with a fourth, fifth, and sixth insisting on their own directions. Like the Balkans in the 1990s, each subnation inside the nation goes to war against the others.

In other words, it is *not* the case that, as a culture becomes increasingly anti-Christian, all the moral issues become clearer. Some do. But knowing how to live and engage in such a culture can become more complex as we're faced with lots of new questions, whether we're talking about resisting school policies on gender pronouns or safety regulations on robots designed for sex. Christians will reach different conclusions amid all these new challenges. Our consciences will respond differently to this and that gray area. Our goal in this booklet has not been to tell you how to respond to any given ethical dilemma ("Do I vote for him or for her?"). Instead, it's to help you know how to respond to those who vote or believe differently, to learn how to make at least some space for them, and to encourage you toward charity and forbearance.

So humbly listen to those who don't share your perspective, especially when they come from a different background. Put yourself in the other person's shoes. What principle of justice are they seeing that you might be missing?

Pray for those you disagree with. When you pray about the outcome of someone else's faith, God often deepens your affection for them. When fellow church members celebrate Bible teachings that are of first importance, jagged-line issues shouldn't overthrow the riches of the truths that we love, live for, and would die for.

Finally, meditate on eternity and the final judgment. This shouldn't cultivate complacency or indifference toward injustice. It should calibrate your political perspective. Measure the *now* according to the eternal *then*. Your hope is not in a platform or party or kingdom now. Your hope is in the day the kingdom of this world becomes the kingdom of our Christ (Rev. 11:15).

How Can Pastors Work for Unity in Politically Divisive Times?

1) Preach expositionally.
2) Continually clarify the distinction between biblical issues and applied-wisdom issues.
3) Continually affirm Christian liberty.
4) Teach forbearance toward the weaker conscience.
5) Point to your church's statement of faith.
6) Speak more to what Scripture says and less on how to accomplish it.
7) Remember that your authority lies with expounding Scripture, not your politics.
8) Practice church discipline.
9) Teach what Scripture says about justice.

10) Teach the congregation to listen and empathize with those from different backgrounds.
11) Publicly pray for the issues causing grief and fear among different parts of the congregation.
12) Don't overestimate the breadth of the problem when only a few people are making noise.
13) Model graciousness toward those who disagree with you.
14) Keep a cool head and don't feel the need to address every issue of the day.
15) Preach the final judgment and sing about heaven often.
16) Preach the gospel every week.

Recommended Resources

If you desire to read longer discussions on these topics written by Jonathan Leeman and Andy Naselli, see the list below.

For Children

Andy Naselli, *That Little Voice in Your Head: Learning about Your Conscience* (Fearn, Scotland: Christian Focus, 2018).

For Church Members

Jonathan Leeman, *How the Nations Rage: Rethinking Faith and Politics in a Divided Age* (Nashville, TN: Nelson, 2018).

Andrew David Naselli and J. D. Crowley, *Conscience: What It Is, How to Train It, and*

Loving Those Who Differ (Wheaton, IL: Crossway, 2016).

For Academics

Jonathan Leeman, *Political Church: The Local Assembly as Embassy of Christ's Rule*, Studies in Christian Doctrine and Scripture (Downers Grove, IL: InterVarsity, 2016).

Jonathan Leeman and Andrew David Naselli, "Politics, Conscience, and the Church: Why Christians Passionately Disagree with One Another over Politics, Why They Must Agree to Disagree over Jagged-Line Political Issues, and How." *Themelios* 43 (May 2020).

Scripture Index

Genesis
9:5–6................. 12

2 Samuel
8:15 12

1 Kings
3:28 19
10:9 12

Proverbs
29:4 12

Matthew
7:16, 20............. 14
15:9 44
16:19................. 31
18:18................. 31

Luke
12:48................. 38

Acts
10:9–16............. 49

Romans
13:1–7 12

14...................... 51
14:1 50
14:1–2 51
14:3–4 52
15:7 51,
                          52

1 Corinthians
15:3 52

Ephesians
2:14 28
2:15 28
4:4–6................. 28

James
1:19–20............. 17
2:18 13
2:19 14

1 Peter
2:9..................... 28

Revelation
11:15................. 58

IX 9Marks

Building Healthy Churches

9Marks exists to equip church leaders with a biblical vision and practical resources for displaying God's glory to the nations through healthy churches.

To that end, we want to see churches characterized by these nine marks of health:

1. Expositional Preaching
2. Biblical Theology
3. A Biblical Understanding of the Gospel
4. A Biblical Understanding of Conversion
5. A Biblical Understanding of Evangelism
6. Biblical Church Membership
7. Biblical Chuch Discipline
8. Biblical Discipleship
9. Biblical Church Leadership

Find all our Crossway titles and other resources at 9Marks.org.